T0072536

The German Immigrants' Story

*Frank and
Eva Miehle*

CAROLYN M. (SOPER) MIEHLE

BALBOA.PRESS

A DIVISION OF HAY HOUSE

Balboa Press books may be ordered through booksellers or by contacting:

Balboa Press
A Division of Hay House
1663 Liberty Drive
Bloomington, IN 47403
www.balboapress.com
844-682-1282

Print information available on the last page.

ISBN: 978-1-9822-7849-6 (sc)
ISBN: 978-1-9822-7848-9 (e)

Balboa Press rev. date: 12/29/2021

Contents

❊

Introduction.. vii
Preface ix

Chapter 1 1
Chapter 2 7
Chapter 3 11
Chapter 4 19
Chapter 5 21
Chapter 6 27
Chapter 7 31
Chapter 8 37
Chapter 9 41
Chapter 10 49
Chapter 11 53
Chapter 12 57

Conclusion 59
Appendix 1 61
Appendix 2 63
Appendix 3 65
Records and photos 67

Introduction

❊

This is a story of German Immigrants, coming to North America early in the 1950's.

One winding tale, filled with many trials and tribulations, drama, heartache and love that prevailed through it all.

This is a story of "Opa and Oma" Miehle, Frank and Eva.

As their daughter-in-law, Carolyn was privileged in spending considerable time in their presence and being interested in the experiences of others, frequently asked Opa to recount different parts of his life. He enjoyed sharing those stories and many afternoons were filled going down memory lane. As a third-generation descendant of British immigrants, the story from another perspective was fascinating to her, due to the extreme diversity.

His filter on the experience may not be that of others, however it is represented, as he recounted it to her, as accurately as possible.

This is not intended to share dirty laundry or offend others. It is, initially, just his perception of events. If others have their view, so be it. As the story progresses, her perception of situations enters the picture, attempting to be presented in the most neutral way possible. Being somewhat removed from the emotional elements of their lives, enabled her to provide more objective observations. She hopes you will find it interesting reading as she found it interesting in hearing and experiencing...

Immigrants to North America brought their skills and the richness of their culture to be shared and enjoyed by all. We are a richer and stronger nations due to their participation, contribution and untiring dedication to the good of all.

A love story....

Preface

❈

The primary focus is on Frank Sr. (Opa)and this is a tribute to his memory. This is a capsulized picture of his life along with his lifelong partner, Eva. Their giving nature and generous hearts will be remembered by many. It is Carolyn's hope that this brief history will be received with the same acceptance felt while in their presence. They were both opinionated, as we all are, however one knew beyond a doubt that their intent was protection and the good for all, from their point of view.

As one views a lovely bouquet of flowers in a patterned vase, from one perspective, you look upon a flower grouping, from afar seeing the blend of hues and you may fail to see the beauty of the pattern of the vase, up close however, one can enjoy not only the beauty of the flowers and the intricate and detailed pattern of the vase, but also the aroma wafting from the blossoms. All views are correct and none more correct than another. All accurate, just different.

All life experience presents a cascade of memories, unfortunately judged and categorized by the beliefs one accumulates from personal experience along with those instilled by parents and one's environment. Since beliefs are made up of thoughts you keep thinking, all perception gets locked into immoveable places that lead to conflict not only on a personal but also a global scale. One example is choice of religion, it seems, it is just geography, based on one's place of birth. None wrong, just different. The human experience is fascinating.

There were so many immigrants during the 1950's, products of conflict in many parts of the world, hoping for a new beginning in a new land.

Chapter 1

❈

F rank (Opa)'s father, Johann, of German descent, was born in Budaors, Hungary in 1875. Many Germans were within the borders of Hungary as the Austro-Hungarian borders shifted many times throughout history. Maria Theresa brought many Germans to Hungary in the 1700's. She encouraged those with trades and they were lured by the gift of land ownership. Those able to clear more land, were given more. Count Esterhasi who lived in Csokvar, not far from Vertesboglar, Opa's birthplace, brought many immigrants in from Baden-Wurttemberg around 1755, to work his property. It is believed the Miehle lineage was in this group.

Johann was a very ambitious man and recognizing that the only way to own land, in his generation, at that time, was ready cash. He decided to immigrate to the US. In July 1900, he entered through Elis Island, New York and worked as a butcher in Chicago and in Sharon, Pennsylvania, returning home with cash to purchase a home and land for his family. He made several trips early in his marriage to Anna Stiftinger. She accompanied him and supported him, hesitantly, in the move, from their homeland. They rented a large house in Sharon, Pennsylvania, with several bedrooms and provided housing for workers from the coal mines. Shifts were day and night, so as one man left a bed, another entered it. Anna was charged with the responsibility of cooking, cleaning and washing for the entire lot, not an easy task. Anna's brother, Ferenz Stiftinger arrived the year before they made their final trip home, returning to Hungary. Opa met Ferenz's son, George, and his wife Mary, from Philadelphia, on one of their trips to Florida and later they travelled to Germany and Hungary with Frank and Carolyn, locating more of the relatives, that remained in Europe.

Frank (Opa) remembers his mother, Anna, saying that she was extremely homesick while in the US, particularly after giving birth and then losing, her first child, Johann,1901. Unfortunately, Anna became quite ill and being pregnant with a second child, begged her husband to return home. They both returned to Hungary in 1905 with Johann (2nd), born 1903, in tow.

Johann purchased a home in a small town about 50 kilometers from Budapest, in Vertesboglar, Kossuth Lajos U. 111. Bela Miehle (son of their second Johann) and Anna(Nagel) still reside in the family home, at time of writing. Johann returned to America three more times, working on farms and in the factories of Sharon, Pennsylvania. Frank recalled his father returning with a great deal of money after each trip. He returned to Hungary permanently in 1912, able to purchase land for a vineyard, and to pay completely, for the family home, which they had purchased from a German family named "Singer". Bela had the purchasing documents in the family Bible in Vertesboglar.

Frank spoke lovingly about his mother, Anna Stiftinger, saying she was an extremely strong individual, tall in stature, having unwavering faith in her four children. Johann (1903), Anna (1905), Frank (1908) and Paul (1918). Their father, being gone so much, didn't have a close relationship with the children and passed away on June 10, 1925. He was kicked in the side of his head by a horse. His health was seriously compromised and he lost sight in one eye. Complications set in later, leading to his demise.

Frank recalled that was very hard for his mother after his father died, raising four children, all high spirited and determined sorts. Their home had a deep lot with a large garden, chickens and pigs, to provide food for the family, with horses to help work the soil. Johann, the eldest son remained in Vertesboglar with his mother, sister and little brother.

Realizing that the small town could not support a second blacksmith, Frank's chosen trade, his mother urged him to move closer to Budapest where he could begin an apprenticeship. Reluctantly leaving his first love in the small town, Frank followed his mother's advice and set out for Budapest at the age of 14. He wrote, in a letter to his cousin, George Stiftinger, "I left home very young. I became a blacksmith apprentice, that I finished. I worked around Budapest suburbs and I was a master-blacksmith. I had my own shop for ten years in the city of Vesces until the Communists sent me out of Hungary to Germany."

Upon arrival in Budapest, staying with relatives, he was put to work, learning his trade. His sense of pride and duty to his mother helped him endure long hours and hard labor. He asked his employer to put all his earnings aside, while he earned extra cash, grooming horses in his free time.

Although by to-day's standards the trip home to Vertesboglar would be minor, at that time, it would require access to a horse, time off from work, with the jeopardy of losing his indenture and of course, money. Trips home didn't happen often and the loneliness weighed heavily upon him. He recounted many times how he had missed his home and particularly his mother in the early years.

The joy he felt when his mother came to see him, dressed in her very best, was remembered by him for the rest of his life. Her trip was a significant one, as she had a special gift to give her son.

She pulled, from the folds of her long skirts, a brown pouch with a draw string at the top and handed it to her son, saying, "This is your dowry, your elder brother will have the farm and with this I hope you can make your beginning." Frank was overwhelmed by her gift, knowing the hardship and sacrifice she had to endure to make this gift possible. This occasion reinforced his determination to succeed and make his mother proud. He finished his apprenticeship confident and strong.

While working, in Vesces, a young man's interest turned to the fairer sex. With Frank's love of singing and music, it followed that dancing was a social event he enjoyed. He participated in a choir and made many friendships there. It happened that a particularly pretty girl caught Frank's eye. She was fun loving and sought after by many. Frank decided to take up the challenge of courtship with Anna Hanek(1915). She was flirtatious by nature and getting her attention was not an easy task. Working long hours made contacts more difficult for him. They dated casually, attending the various festivals held throughout the year. Feeling her wishes could be imposed on Frank, she met with resistance, as he was also a very strong-willed individual. She would send notes with her sister, Eva, conveying what she wanted. Not being swayed by her fantasies, and not pleased by her flirtatious nature with other young men, conflict arose and Frank took note of the quieter nature of her sister, much more co-operative and more to his liking. Thus began their interaction. Eva kept their secret from Anna for some time, until it was revealed that they were serious about the nature of their courtship.

Eva's parents, John and Anna(Kellner) lived on the main street in Vesces and Anna, their daughter, had a small shop at the front of the home where she sold candy and dry goods. Their younger brother, Joe (1930) spent a considerable time with Anna, going on deliveries. Anna, basically became a mother figure for Joe. This was a great help, as their mother suffered from Parkinson's. Much of the mother's care and household responsibilities, fell on Eva's shoulders in the early years.

Eva, proudly announced to her family that she, had a gentleman's interest. Silence fell on the room and Anna's temper flared, angry that she was being passed over for her sister. The family fell quiet as Anna went into her rage, a common event when all was not going the way she wished. As she raced around the room, she came upon a knife and threw it at Eva, cutting her arm. Opa Hanek stepped in, separating the tormented Anna from the shocked and hurt Eva.

So began Frank and Eva's courtship.

Anna lived with a Hungarian military man and a German fighter pilot, later marrying Helmut Oswald, a business man and member of the SS. He carried the tattooed number under his arm verifying his affiliation. He never spoke of his war experience, however did indicate on one occasion, that choice was not an option for anyone during those times. Fortunately, his duties were bookkeeping, in the background of activities during the WW II. Everyone was aware of his affinity to alcohol. One can read into that whatever they wish. What he experienced was never revealed.

Anna was a generous aunt that supported her sister, her brother and their children for many years. She stepped up and became a tremendous support for her parents for the rest of their lives. Both parents lived with Anna and Helmut in Reichenbach, Germany until they passed.

Chapter 2

---　✜　---

F rank and Eva were married Jan.20,1934 in Vesces. After the wedding they lived for a short time in Eva's parents' home, Fo 69, along with Anna and Joe, a situation that needed to change needless to say.

A property became available down the street from the Hanek home, and Frank purchased it for 12,000 Bengo. The talk was, that he had over extended himself and he would never pay for it. Undaunted, Frank pushed forward, with Eva by his side. He went to his past employer and collected all the back wages set aside for him during his apprenticeship and along with the money from his mother, was able to reduce the amount owing significantly. He set up his own blacksmith shop behind the house and hired three apprentices.

Frank and Eva worked long hours carving out a life for themselves. The glad news of the upcoming birth of their first child, added to their joy. Frank was born healthy and for all intents and purposes, his future looked good. Unfortunately, fate had something else in store. He died due to "crib death" at two months of age. Both Frank and Eva were devastated. Soon after, Eva became pregnant again and gave birth to another son, Frank John, March 18,1936. This son thrived and was joyously received into the family. During this period of their life, Frank worked from sun up to sun down, forging horseshoes and wagon wheels.

He would make extra horseshoes of all different sizes and Frank John, said he remembered them hanging neatly in rows from the beams of the attic. In addition, he forged extra wagon wheels, the metal fitting over the wooden frames, used at the time. All were there for rapid retrieval, facilitating prompt service whenever someone needed service. His reputation grew, for fast and efficient service.

In his thirties, Frank decided he would upgrade his skills in animal husbandry and going to Budapest, learned the diseases and treatments for various conditions that afflicted the horses. Others laughed at him, going to school at his age. Not dissuaded, he continued, determined to provide complete service in his growing business. He cleaned and dressed the wounds found in the horses' hooves. Many conditions, when not attended to properly, meant putting the horse down, way before its time. He became trusted by his customers and all prospered.

During all this time, Eva was tending to chickens, a large garden, cooking, baking, cleaning and washing for her family and the three live-in apprentices. Should she want chicken for dinner, first she had to kill it, clean it and then prepare it. Two chickens served for one meal. Ferenz Herczig, Frank's sister Anna's, son, apprenticed under Frank and spoke highly of Eva's meals and regrettably found Frank to be a very hard taskmaster. His expectation was that the apprentices should work just as hard as he did...wielding a hammer from dawn to dust... Their home became a center of activity day and night, with customers coming and going at all hours, with Frank Jr. playing underfoot... Rest came only on Sundays.

Their son, Frank Jr, also a lover of music, remembered lying in bed Sunday mornings with his parents, singing songs with his father. Second melody came naturally to both of them.

Frank Sr. sang in a choir, in Hungary and continued this enjoyment for the rest of his life.

Frank Jr., their boy, recalled his childhood, taking a wagon, made for him by his father, and upon his mother's request, wheeling unbaked loaves of rye bread, down to the bakery. Later in the day she would call him to fetch the baked loaves, bringing them home. His reward was a fresh, warm heel of bread smeared with pork lard and sprinkled with paprika.

Reports were that this child was going to be a dreamer, having time on his hands, he would follow the pig herder out to the fields with the family dog, Boobie and there would pass time, watching the fish and frogs in the water hole and the small stream that flowed by.

When a pig was slaughtered, they fashioned a soccer ball, using the bladder of the pig. Thus began Frank Jr.'s love of the game. Later, his father would reward him every school year end with a real, brand-new ball, providing his report was favorable. Frank Jr. was envied in the neighborhood, having a real soccer ball each year.

Six years after Frank's birth, Eva was expecting her third child, John, born Feb. 2,1942. The relationship with Eva's family was amiable but distant. She continued to help her parents living a few houses down whenever she could, particularly if Anna was unavailable. Following Eva's marriage Anna stepped up and filled a vital role in supporting their parents and caring for her younger brother, Joe. Anna continued with her business and Joe would help her. Peaceful routines seemed to begin to prevail but not for long...

The war years changed everything.

Chapter 3

— ❈ —

F rank was busier than ever as activity and productivity was important for the war effort. The family's dilemma arose. Being of German descent, in a Hungarian city, they were not alone and the lines of battle and alliances were drawn. Since communications were limited, most were unaware of world affairs, busy just making a living. A speaker came to the choir practice one evening and after listening to him, the entire group was classified as part of the Hitler movement. This further divided the community since Hungarians were also singers in the choir. Neighbor began to turn against neighbor.

Frank Sr.'s notice to serve in the German army was received and they knew their lives would change forever.

Before following the order, Frank served their family in another way. John, their youngest, developed a growth under his jaw, a boil on the side of his neck. At the time the local doctor thought the growth was of little concern and said it would likely go away. Not confident with this assurance, the family travelled by wagon to Budapest. A specialist there, recognized that it needed to be lanced right away and that John's life was in danger. He lost a significant amount of blood. For a two-year-old, this was a traumatic experience to say the least. After testing the entire family, it was ascertained that Frank Sr.'s blood was a match. John remained in the Budapest hospital, with specialist supervision, receiving a pint of blood from his father daily. The family made the trip back and forth in an effort to save him. Frank John remembers his brother, crying from his crib in the hospital, as they left, saying, "I want to go home. (Ich will heim gehe)" The specialist instructed Frank Sr. to replenish his blood by drinking red wine, just enough to feel good, but not become intoxicated. The ordeal weakened Frank significantly, however served to bring his son back to good health. They were told due to the age difference between donor and recipient, the child would grow to have a large stature. This prediction bore true as John became a large, gentle, very tall man.

In service in the army, Frank was initially assigned the duties of a sharp shooter as his skill and accuracy qualified him, however he was not deployed to that duty since his mechanical skills were deemed more useful in maintaining equipment, behind the lines. It was fortunate, as sharp shooters were the first line and met their demise early in combat.

Initially, the Hungarians aligned with Germany, switched sides as Russia began its movement into Hungary and its occupation there. With the Hungarians aligned with the Russians and the Allies, Germans within Hungary were soon captured and sent to prison. Frank was imprisoned in Poland, where treatment was, as it is in any war, limited food, and physical beatings were common place. Once again, his skill in repairs provided a small reprieve, as the Russians advanced into Hungary, their equipment also needed frequent repair and Frank was moved to a prison, just outside Budapest. Here they lived on one bowl of bean soup per day. From this location he was transported on weekends, to his own shop, where he was forced to work as a laborer repairing Russian machinery. The building, that housed prisoners, still stands next to the bridge on the Buda side of the Danube. It was a relief for the family to know that their father was indeed alive.

Fearing the unknown, Frank and Eva felt unsafe in Vesces, since it was so close to the Budapest airport and it was being bombed on a regular basis. They assumed that they would need to abandon their home temporarily and possibly return after the war, should they survive. Under this assumption, they dug large holes in the back yard and hid containers of salted meat covered in lard, along with flasks of wine, anticipating their need for food upon their return. A return that was quite different from their expectations.

On one of the weekends home, he informed Eva that he and two of his friends planned to escape the following weekend and requested that she put together small provisions to assist them. Fearful but obedient, Eva kept their secret and the following weekend, Frank and his two friends left, under the cover of darkness, trying to make their way to the Austrian border. Riding rail by night and sleeping under cover by day, they soon were within reach of the border. While hiding in a farmer's barn, they were discovered. Fortunately, it was autumn and the farmer was in dire need of help with his crops. On the promise that they would help him bring in all the crops they were housed and fed, staying in the barn for safety. In payment, the farmer promised to assist them with the border crossing. When the work was completed, the farmer, hid them in a hay wagon, making it past a number of checkpoints. At the last one, they were discovered and surprising the patrols, made a run for the border which was in sight. Frank recounted seeing bullets knit the ground in front of them. They were fortunate not being hit. One shouted that they should surrender, the reply was, "Then they will shoot us for sure." They kept on running to safety. Frank spoke many times of the sound of the bullets and the luck they had. Free once again, but hungry and tired, they set out to find work, food and shelter. Austria being neutral, was safe haven for many escapees.

Unaware whether her husband was dead or alive, Eva started to prepare to evacuate their home. Bombs fell regularly nearby. Frank Jr. spoke of playing in the craters created by the blasts. As soon as they heard the whine of aircraft overhead, Eva would coral the two boys and hide in the root cellar, until the threat had passed.

Eva and Frank's possessions and property after years of hard work included their home furnished, comfortably. Their front room was furnished with high gloss cherrywood bedroom furniture used only by special guests. Engraved glass doors closed this special room from the rest of the house. ...everything would be left behind. Over time Frank had acquired plots of land where he had planted white and red grapes for wine making.

It was with a heavy heart that Eva packed up meagre belongings to join her sister, Anna, her brother, Joe and Oma and Opa Hanek, as they set out in an open wagon to head to relatives in Vertesboglar. Being some distance from the bombing, it was felt to be a much safer place. They left the family dog, Boobie, tied at the house, knowing he was another mouth to feed. Along route, looking back they saw the dog running to catch up and he then hid under the wagon, likely fearing he might be left behind again. He stayed under the wagon until they reached Vertesboglar. They arrived safely and stayed approximately three months with relatives.

There was limited room for them and they did not wish to jeopardize the safety of relatives, so moved on with a group of people heading for Austria. Anna left the group and joined her friend not making the last part of the trip with the family. Boobie stayed on the farm in Vertesboglar enjoying a warm happy home. They made their way by horse and wagon, along with the Wirt family, to Austria, and stayed in a castle in Rapps on the Thyai near the Austrian-Czech border. Frank remembered the castle and they visited it on one of their trips to Austria years later. The family remained in the castle for about a year, fed by the generosity of the local people of the town. They all slept on the floors of a large hall. Frank said that winter there, was enjoyable for a child of nine, sleigh riding down the road, flanked on one side by the castle and a steep slope that went down to the river on the other. Using pieces of cardboard as sleighs, there was a group of children, all experiencing the same predicament.

They returned to Hungary, when they heard the fighting had subsided in the spring of 1945. The control of Hungary had been handed to the Russians by the Allies, and being German, their problems were far from over. On the trek home, Russian soldiers stole their two horses exchanging them for a pregnant mare and a donkey. They also helped themselves to anything they desired of their possessions. They had no choice but to comply.

Arriving back, after over a year away, they found the home was empty, ram sacked, windows broken, all furniture was gone. Their backyard was mounds of dirt where their stores had been, all raided. Dead chickens, killed from the force of the bombing, were scattered in the yard. Food was shared by those that had some with those that had none. Frank Jr. remembered sleeping on the floor boards of their empty house.

Neighbors turned on neighbors and no one could be trusted, as alliances were unknown. Hungarians, as reported by Eva, sided with the Russians, as the occupying force, and Germans were second class citizens and were called "bitte schwabs", certainly unwelcome on Hungarian soil.

Skinny chickens, once caught, would make a large pot of soup. Flour became a staple as noodles filled stomachs. Eva aged quickly, overwhelmed with worry for her husband and the protection of her boys. The first wave of Russian occupation was particularly hostile as theft, rape and beatings were frequent. Russian soldiers, intoxicated, raped many women and Frank remembered shouting for "Patrol, Patrol" when some came to the neighborhood. Young girls slept out in the fields for their protection, since they were targets on such occasions. All the men were gone and old people, women and children remained.

In the spring of 1946, a bell ringer announced a notice posted on the town hall and the people named on the list were to report to the train station. Their names were on the list. It was said that those in the men's choir were Nazi sympathizers. Along with those that had housed German youths in the 1930's. Frank remembered the boy assigned to their home, sent due to the fact there was so little food in Germany at that time. They were told to report to the train station for their departure, destination unknown.

With very few possessions, women, children and old people boarded box cars and awaited the knowledge of the destination, Germany or Siberia. As good fortune would have it, the train they were on, headed west toward Germany. It stopped periodically, just enough time to disembark, go to the bathroom, if lucky, dig up potatoes from a neighboring field with their hands, eat them and promptly vomit. On occasion they were able to make a quick fire to cook them and rush back on board when the engine started gearing up once again. They reassured each other, at the time, that this also would be temporary and that they would return in a year or so. At each of these stops Eva combed the area making inquiries about the three Germans from Vesces that may have passed this way. At long last, in Austria, someone heard of three Germans meeting their description and the family was happily reunited again.

Germans, not on the list at city hall, returning from the war, to Hungary, were sent to work in the mines in Siberia, returning to families for brief periods. The only way they would be allowed to stay with their families permanently would be if they "Hungarianized" their names. Frank's godfather was one such individual. Their German name was "Strohmeier" and when changed, their new name became "Szabados. His godfather was not required to leave home again. Frank and Carolyn visited their home in the 70's and they proudly showed them a large clock that had been gifted to them by Frank and Eva, as a wedding gift, so many years before.

Frank and Eva lost all their possessions due to the war, their home, his blacksmith shop and their vineyards, with no compensation. Frank and Carolyn inquired about the properties, years later, after hearing that some families were receiving ownership once again. They went to the authorities, while in Hungary, and were told that they should have been there the year before when the package had been announced, in the Hungarian newspapers. They had wanted to gift the property on the main street to Bela's son, as he was a mechanic and the location would have been perfect for setting up his own shop.

Other families such as the Strifler family were torn apart. Adam, Frank's friend, remembered running, as a ten- year-old in 1946, after the train, that took his mother away to Russia, never to be seen again.

There was a great deal of family suffering on all sides. Common folk unfortunately get caught up in the strife created by governments, both then and now.

Chapter 4

※

In Germany, displaced Germans or relocated Germans were not really welcomed by their fellow Germans as their lot was also that of hardship. They were called "Ruchsac Deutsche", backpack Germans. However, Germany repatriated many Hungarian Germans following the war. The family reunited, was housed in barracks in a small town of Denkendorf, near Stuttgart. Frank recalls the barracks, as flea infested. Women sewed feed bags together, filled them with straw for blankets. Each morning these were shaken out with dust flying everywhere. Work for the men gradually was found and Frank Sr. began working once again. While in the barracks they were given carrot soup, which when offered to the dogs, was left uneaten. Daily rations of one slice of bread per person, were provided, and that, Frank and Eva often gave to their sons.

The government went around the town and assigned families to be taken in by their citizens. The Miehle family, Frank, Eva and the boys were assigned to the Straus family on Zeppelin Strasse, being allowed to occupy two rooms in their small home. Life began to take on some form of routine. Although not truly accepted by the other neighborhood children, Frank Jr. found his niche playing soccer.

Having lost two years of school due to the war, a tutor was arranged for Frank and he soon caught up to his peers. He attended the large school building in the center of town, which still stands at the time of writing. There is an artesian well in front of the school, that perpetually brings forth fresh water for the use of passersby. John was four years of age at this time, born in 1942. Eva worked her creative powers and the family enjoyed many delicious meals once again, savored more now that they had a space to themselves. John started school there in Denkendorf. Frank Sr. was able to obtain better housing in an eight-family house at the base of the hill entering Denkendorf. Frank Jr., at the age of 15, began his electrician apprenticeship, travelling by train to Esslingen.

Recognizing the boys' musical ability, Frank saved enough money to buy their sons their first accordions and lessons began. Frank Jr. recalled wearing it strapped on his back while riding a bicycle up and down the hills of the town. He was skilled and a quick study and was assigned the task of providing entertainment for his parents and their friends every Sunday afternoon. He would have preferred time with his friends, however complied with his parents' wishes. Frank Sr. started making his own wine, which he sold cheaply to friends and neighbors. Their home seemed to Frank Jr. to be a central gathering place. The men would join in and sing all the favorite melodies known from their past. It was here they lived, until setting out for North America. The high cost of land in Germany deterred Frank from starting again in Germany and the land of opportunity awaited across the ocean. Times and the economy in Germany were also very difficult and the lure of the west beckoned Frank Sr. to move on.

Frank Sr. suggested Australia to the family and he met clear resistance, considering such a distant destination.

Applications were prepared to immigrate to the USA and to Canada. The Canadian papers came in first, soon followed by the US papers. Since they knew people in Canada, that was their choice.

Chapter 5

❈

The decision was made for Frank to leave prior to bringing the family, since he only had funds for the fare for one person. He would get established, then send word and money for them to follow. The conditions were, if you could pay your fare, you could choose your destination. If the Canadian government covered your fare, you could be sent wherever they decided, many going west to work on the farms.

He arrived, aboard the Arosa Kulm, at Pier 21, in Halifax, was processed and boarded a train for Niagara Falls. He had seven dollars in his pocket. In Niagara Falls, with the address of the Schankula family in his hand, he motioned to the taxi driver that he wanted to be taken there. Arriving at his destination, a distance of about three miles from the train station, he held out his money with the belief the driver would take the appropriate fare. Needless to say, that was the last he saw of his money. The Schankula family housed Frank for a short period of time and brought him to find work as a brick layer's helper and later at Norton Steel. Mr. Schankula had worked for Frank, while in Vesces, in the blacksmith shop, and he was pleased to help his friend.

Losing everything in Hungary, Frank arrived in Germany in 1946, at 38 years of age, starting from nothing. Then once again, in Canada, at age 45, in 1953, with pockets that were empty. He found a small apartment in Niagara Falls, which he rented, and made arrangements for Eva and the boys to join him in the fall. He was able to save the $700 needed for the family's fare to Canada.

Meanwhile, Eva, still in Germany, had worked hard keeping the family together and food on the table. Frank forwarded money to her as frequently as he could.

She readied herself and the boys for the long voyage to Canada. They boarded the Italian freighter, the Costal Bianco, September 18, 1953. A friend, Mr. Gonauer, built a wooden truck for them to fill with what provisions they could fit, for their new adventure. They set sail on the seven-day crossing of the Atlantic, leaving from Bremen Hoffen, in northern Germany. The ship was sixteen tons, relatively small by to-day's standards and it rolled considerably on route. Frank recalled, seventeen years old at the time, that the dining room was filled the first day and everyone enjoyed the food. This changed drastically as more and more passengers became seasick. It seemed the children were least affected, perhaps since they seldom sat still. Many parents found it a challenge to keep them in tow, while at the same time suffering the ills of the trip. Mrs. Bauer had double trouble with her son, young Michael, as he was running wild. Following him, her hand was slammed by the heavy cabin door as the boat heaved with the waves.

At long last, they reached Halifax, entering at Pier 21, as Frank Sr. had done earlier in the year. After processing, they boarded a train for Niagara. Frank Jr. recalled the train ride, viewing the country side thinking, "Why did they come to such a barren land?" They stayed in the small apartment for a short time until they moved to a small home, 5717 Dunn Street, not far from the Panasonic

Tower. Upon arrival, Frank Jr. recalled his father having purchased quite a variety of different foods to celebrate. That was the first time he had seen or tasted bananas, and didn't really care for them, on first impression. Here they settled in once again and life began to develop a routine.

Frank recalled his father's disappointment when asked to contribute $100 toward the construction of St Thomas More Catholic Church on Dorchester Road. The individual pressured him to submit the entire amount. Frank told him he could give him $10 per week to help out, however having just landed and bringing his family to Canada, could not afford that large sum of money. Still pressuring him for the full amount, Frank decided that church attendance would not be needed and they never went again. Since the lack of consideration, he felt, was not appropriate.

Fortunately, work was steady, with regular income, along with Eva's creative skills cooking, life became normal once again. Frank Sr. was able to arrange the continuation of Frank Jr.'s electrical training with a small contractor, Mike Repa. Here the challenge of learning a new language was met and overcome relatively quickly, as tools were the same and he was a quick study in this area as well. He attended night school for a short time, however found it boring as lessons moved too slowly, in his opinion, and he stopped going after two months. Frank Sr. went to work for Ontario Hydro as welder in the tunnels. (The project was started in 1954, to divert water to SAB 2, a second generating station). With this employment, having considerable overtime, he was able to save enough money to begin building a new home for his family, 6390 Atlee Street. Borrowing money was not part of his nature and he exchanged labor with various trades to complete the home to his specifications.

About the same time, Frances Wittman immigrated to Canada, a young seventeen-year-old, a shy and quiet individual. Her family background was disrupted, but not as tumultuous as the Miehle experience, with regard to the war years. Her parents sent her to Canada, hoping for a better life for their daughter with the plan that they would follow at a later time. Her sister, Theresa and her husband, Joe Bayer arrived shortly afterward. Fortunately, Frances acquired live-in employment with Dr. Brown on Victoria Avenue, cooking and doing light housework as well as assisting with their children. Those years were very lonely for her and she missed Germany desperately.

Frank Jr. found Canadian girls paid little attention to new Canadians, especially those that didn't own a car. Frank started dating Frances. The Hungarian Germans tended to mix together helping each other whenever possible. When their relationship became serious, his parents clearly expressed their displeasure with the union, since Frank was only 19 and Frances was 20 years of age at the time. However, a child was on the way and they were married May 1955. Frank Sr. would not attend the wedding as he was so upset with the situation. Unfortunately, their married life began with them living in the Miehle home until, Frank Jr. found a small upstairs apartment for his wife and son, Frankie, on Dunn Street. They later found a somewhat larger one on Ash Street. Fortunately, with time and the joy Frankie brought the family, fences were gradually mended. Frank was also dreaming of building a new home for his young family, just as his father had done. He was able to purchase a lot on Warden Avenue for $800.00. Weekends, he would wire homes for fellow countrymen, carpenters, bricklayers, all engaged in the same pursuit. The exchange of labor was money saving for all involved. True bartering in action.

Frank also played accordion with Merstorff's band Saturday nights, as well as practicing and playing soccer. His love of the game was also instilled in his young son at a very early age. He had his new family home, 7067 Warden Avenue, completed in 1959. Their lives were very busy and happy. (Interestingly, at the present time, Angelica Seibert, granddaughter of Mr. and Mrs. Gonauer, owns the home now, the same Gonauer, that built the travel trunk for Eva's journey in 1953.)

Both Eva and Frances found work at the Refectory, in the kitchen, down by the Falls, during the summer months.

Meanwhile, Frank and Eva were contacted by her brother, Joe and his wife, Maria (Mitzi), living in Germany. They wanted to immigrate to Canada and needed sponsors. Frank and Eva agreed to help them out and had them live with them for a year after arrival. They contributed $20 per week for their room and board until they were ready to strike out on their own. Joe and Mitzi purchased a home across the street from Frank and Frances' home, living there until the mid-60's.

Chapter 6

❋

F rank Sr., always the opportunist, felt that USA offered more than Canada and filled out the necessary documentation to make a move to Ohio. When the papers arrived, Frank, Eva and John set out for Cleveland, Ohio in 1960. John had tried his hand in body work on cars in Canada and this activity was interrupted with the move. Fortunately, John found work in Cleveland in a Twist and Drill Company, where he worked his entire career. John also loved soccer, being a strong player and talented referee. He was very active with the Donauschwaben Club in Cleveland, later named Concordia Soccer Club. (located at 7370 Columbia Rd. Olmstead Falls, Ohio). Having fallen in love with Elisabeth Huber and concerned about single men being called up for the war in Viet Nam, she and John were married in November 1963.

In 1961-62 Frank and Frances were experiencing marital difficulties, as she was still very homesick for her parents in Germany. It was suggested that a child would help Frances feel happier and the decision was made to have another child. A healthy baby girl, Susan Anita was born Oct. 16, 1963. Frank recalled the difficult trip to Cleveland as he, Frances, Frankie and one month old, Susan, were caught in a bad snowstorm, trying to attend his brother's wedding. He had been asked to be the best man for the ceremony.

Frank and Eva purchased a home on Lloyd Road in Cleveland and over time gradually owned a total of three homes on that same street, renting them to assist with mortgage payments. Frank and Eva were very generous and enjoyed entertaining in their home. Eva enjoyed babysitting her two lovely granddaughters Tina and Tammy. With steady employment as a welder, Frank continued to thrive financially. He was employed by Harold Schott, who owned ball bearing factories in various places. He took to Frank, as he demonstrated hard, devoted effort in whatever task was set before him.

Frank continued his participation in a men's choir and he and Eva enjoyed weekend dances at the German Club in Cleveland.

Back in Canada, Frances, still longed to return to Germany since her parents had remained there. Quite often expressing homesickness, Frank suggested that she and Susan take a trip to see her parents, hoping this would calm her anxieties. It so happened that George and Doris Mayer was taking the same flight to visit his relatives in Austria. George reported that Frances had a great deal of difficulty managing Susan, an energetic four-year-old, throughout the flight. Frank had noticed similar problems as he would find the child dressed in summer clothes on very cold days and when questioned about her attire, Frances' response was, "It was what she wanted to wear." It seemed that Frances was unable to handle Susan. Frankie kept to himself, sensitive to his mother's difficulties and many times was hurt by her outbursts. Fortunately, he had an outlet, as he was busy with hockey, soccer and spending time with friends. While Frances and Susan were away, Frank painted the entire inside of the house, giving it a facelift, hoping Frances would be pleased upon their return. Returning, little had changed, nothing seemed to lift her spirits. Frank solicited the help of her sister, Theresa and later wrote to her parents to come to Canada for an extended visit. Susan was very attached to her father and would accompany him to the hockey arena and soccer games, both his games and those of her brother, Frankie. She was dubbed a rink rat since she explored every nook and cranny of the building, free as a bird.

Frances' parents arrived and seeing the condition of their daughter, decided it best for her to return with them to Germany, leaving behind her husband and children. Apparently, as reported by Frank, they told her she wasn't a mother to the children, nor a wife to her husband. Frank legalized all the separation papers along with child custody documents. Property was evaluated and Frances returned to Germany with half of their accumulated assets. It was necessary for him to obtain a loan from Dieter Schutz in order to provide the lump sum required. Frank was pleased that the children stayed with him and he found it a challenge to manage everything. Fortunately, he was able to obtain after school support, with Mathilda Blaich, the wife of a soccer buddy, Willi, that lived nearby.

Frank and Eva, realizing the dilemma their son was in, with Frances gone, suggested that he and the children join them in Cleveland. Frank agreed with them and the applications for entering the US were filed. Susan was five and Frankie was thirteen at the time.

Frank met and later, married Carolyn Soper in 1974. Their paths crossed while he was working on the construction site at a school in Fort Erie, where she taught Grade one. Sharing the news of the new relationship, with his parents, brought happiness, as the challenge of raising young children for them, while in their sixties, could have been managed, but would not have been an easy task. As a result of the new developments, the move to Cleveland was not completed, although the papers did arrive, and that enabled Frank to obtain work in the US, when construction was slow in Canada.

Chapter 7

— ❈ —

F rank and Eva took three trips back to Germany and one to Hungary. They visited Anna and her husband Helmut, living in Reichenbach, Germany. Eva had given Anna her Hanek inheritance since Anna generously and caringly attended to both of their parents until they passed away.

In 1979, Anna and Helmut came to the US and Canada for a visit. Arriving in Cleveland, they travelled by car with her brother, Joe, up to Niagara to visit Frank and Carolyn. The plan was to stay with them and drive further north to their cottage on Bear Lake, Parry Sound District. Before leaving, Frank had a soccer game on Saturday, a particularly hot day. Tante Anna loved sitting in the sun and enjoyed watching the game that afternoon. The next morning although not feeling quite herself, she insisted on making the trip north to see the cottage. Upon arrival there, she became quite ill and was taken to the hospital. It was determined that she had the flu. Since she was not well throughout that night, Joe decided to return to Cleveland as quickly as possible. He and Mitzi took Tante Anna to Cleveland Clinic where they confirmed the flu diagnosis, returning to Joe's home with medications. She did not improve and returning once again to the Cleveland Clinic, it was determined that she had suffered multiple minor strokes and she passed away there.

Uncle Helmut was at a loss as to what to do as he wanted to return her remains to Germany. He knew that she would have wanted to be buried next to her parents, in Reichenbach. After considerable red tape, he returned home with her coffin on the same flight.

Frank and Carolyn visited her grave site later on a trip to Germany, staying with Uncle Helmut. It was difficult while there as he begged them to move to Germany to take care of him with the promise that they would inherit their home. Knowing that they could not uproot the family, the move would not be possible. This trip was five years after Tante Anna had passed and he still had her shoes by the door and apron hanging in the kitchen. Those were difficult years for him. Fortunately, his son from his first marriage, living in Germany was available for support, along with his former wife. Uncle Helmut was a jovial sort, however enjoyed alcohol and his rosy cheeks and big smile were evidence when he was particularly mellow. Family had many pleasant visits with them over the years.

Frank and Eva enjoyed many happy years in Cleveland with minor aches and pains. Frank developed kidney stones and found that cold weather was definitely not to his liking. Once again, as Eva put it, "He has wander shoes again."

Visiting friends in Florida, Frank and Eva, made an offer on a four-unit apartment complex on 18th Avenue in Fort Lauderdale. Eva initially was not pleased with the quick decision, as she would be away from John and Betty's two girls, to whom she was very attached. The decision was made and they returned to Cleveland and put their properties up for sale.

The final move south happened in 1973, the same year Frankie, their grandson, received a soccer scholarship to attend Cleveland State University.

Frank went to his employer, Harold Schott, (uncle to Margie Schott, former part owner of the Cleveland Browns) telling him that he would no longer be in his employ. Harold told him, "If you are moving south, I will too, provided you take care of my place in Florida for me." Frank agreed that he would help him out, not really believing he meant what he said. Sure enough, the following year, Harold called him up telling him he had purchased a property in Golden Beach, in the northeast corner of Miami-Dade. He arrived later that year and took them to see the property. It was a large home, with five bedrooms and seven bathrooms, on the intercoastal with a big lawn and hedges and a four-car garage. Frank would go twice a month to cut the grass and keep the grounds in order while Eva cleaned and prepared the house for Harold's intermittent visits with family and friends. Knowing when he would be coming, she would prepare a selection of her delicious baked goods which he always enjoyed. One March break, when Frank and Carolyn were in Florida, they went with Frank and Eva to Harold's place to help out. Harold was entertaining the Governor of Ohio and Eva provided a wide selection of her homemade treats. Harold paid them $700 per month. They found this to be a benefit along with the income from their apartment rental income. Eva was a very forthright individual and spoke her mind. Coming into one of the bedrooms at Harold's place she surprised a lady on the floor doing exercises. Eva's comment to her was, "You work hard enough, you no need exercise".

Frank, with a good nose for opportunity, found a two-bedroom, two-bathroom, single family house, not far from the apartments, 5260 NE 18th Terrace. The benefit of this location was that Eva could start a large garden, which she took great pride in. There were banana trees and a large mango tree in the backyard. Together they planted an orange tree and a grapefruit tree. After a visit with them one's car would be loaded for the trip home.

Frank and Eva, found the German Club in Fort Lauderdale and he joined a men's choir there, about 30 strong, led by Lydia King. All the men loved Lydia King. She knew exactly how to manage the group and concerts were a frequent occurrence. She dressed in lovely flowing gowns with frequent changes during the concert, singing solo with an adoring back up choir.

Harold Schott also purchased an orange grove in Florida, somewhat inland. Frank (Opa) and Eva (Oma) were invited to help themselves to oranges as often as they wished. When visiting, it was a requirement that a visit to the orange grove was on the schedule and bushels of oranges were brought back. On one occasion, Eva, dumped oranges in the trunk of Frank and Carolyn's car, not thinking about the frost they would experience returning to Canada. On route, it was necessary to clear out the trunk and bring all the oranges in bags into the motel on the trip home, just so they wouldn't freeze overnight. They were delicious ripened on the tree, much better than those purchased in the north. Eva made mango jam using up the bumper crop the tree always yielded and would give it away to any visitors coming by. Both Frank and Eva were generous beyond measure.

They went to a small park, just off Oakland Park Boulevard, fondly labelled Opa's beach, meeting their friends, sitting in the shade of the trees and enjoying good conversation usually about three times a week, when not required to tend to Harold's property. On one occasion, Frank mentioned to Harold that he didn't want to drive all the way to Golden Beach since it was wearing out his car. Harold's response was, "When you come up to Cleveland, I will buy you a new one." Although hard to believe, Frank took him up on his offer and sure enough, Harold purchased a brand-new Buick for them, which Frank used for many years. He gave his older car to Frankie, just beginning university, and that was greatly appreciated.

The twenty years they lived in Florida were the best years, as they were busy, but not as demanding, on either one of them, physically, compared to their early history. They teased each other and their home was a welcoming place for everyone. It seemed they had finally received the rewards after so many years of difficulty. For many years, they would drive from Florida to Cleveland and continue on to Canada, to keep in touch with friends and relatives.

Annual trips to Florida are remembered as including excursions to the farmers' fields to pick tomatoes and peppers, meals that overloaded the dining room table and relaxing evenings, taking walks and watching TV. An outing to the German Club at night, usually included a meal, dancing to traditional music and perhaps a medley of songs presented by the men's choir. Lydia King's medley of songs were always well received and at times could bring a tear to many an eye.

While Frank and Carolyn were visiting one Christmas in Florida, Opa received a phone call asking if he was the Frank Miehle, the son of Anna Stiftinger. Curious, but pleased, his first cousin, George Stiftinger and his wife, Mary, from Philadelphia, were involved in investigating the family tree. They were actively tracking down the relatives that they could find, living in America. They invited any Miehle's that were available to attend a family reunion in Sharon, Pennsylvania, the following summer. That reunion was such a treat for Opa, as George was fascinated in all the family details. George and Mary had travelled to Europe previously trying to locate relatives, however not speaking German or Hungarian, they had been unsuccessful in obtaining all the information they were hoping for.

It was suggested that Frank and Carolyn travel with them, the following year, to Vertesboglar and Vesces, since Frank was fluent in both Hungarian and German. During that trip, George was thrilled to visit the old homestead and Bela Miehle, son of Johann Miehle, Opa's elder brother. He assisted them tremendously, since he had lived there all his life. Bela had been the town's mayor, a retired school principal, and was also fascinated with family history. It was here that so much of this story was revealed. Bela, having researched the family name, found out that their surname was Mille, in the 1761. In some church records, he found another spelling Mihle. (1790). The parents, Mille, were born in Germany, while their first-born son Josephur was born in Hungary, since they immigrated there. The male line is as follows: Joannes Mille May 1761, Josephur Mihle/Mille April 17, 1790, Josephus Mille Nov. 8,1826, Gyorgy Mille March 28, 1847, Johannes Mille/Miehle Jan. 24 1875. (Opa's father).

Chapter 8

※

I n Florida, Oma and Opa would usually have projects that needed tending, such as planting trees, picking mangos and repairing the screened in porch. One year's memorable activity was trapping an opossum family that had taken up living in the attic. They had entered in through a vent under the eaves over the porch roof and one could clearly hear them scurrying about, on the ceiling over the bedrooms. Since Opa was hard of hearing, they were only detected upon one of Frank and Carolyn's visits. They were able to acquire a trap, bait it with cat food, and were successful in safely transferring the family to a nearby park. The opossum was not a happy camper, snarling at them, peaceful only when the cage was covered with an old blanket. One exciting evening..

Opa seemed to depend on Frank's opinion more and more as time passed. Together, they purchased a Buick Century which he drove until losing his license due to cataract surgery and severe hearing difficulties. The many years using a hammer and anvil as a blacksmith, without ear protection, took its toll. Oma would mutter her complaints about him, in the kitchen out of ear shot.

Dependence had also increased as they requested assistance preparing documents for income tax, explaining notices from the city and accompanying them to various doctor appointments as well as sorting out medications and ointments. Oma was unable to read or write English or German, Hungarian being her educational background.

Frank (Opa) developed eye problems, which created some issues for them since Eva (Oma) had never learned to drive. Their close friends, the Neuhoffer's helped with doctor appointments along with their daughter, Gerda Zeitz. Frank, Carolyn, Susan and sometimes, Frankie would spend their Christmases with Oma and Opa. They started to pressure Frank and Carolyn to move south, to help them out. This was a big decision, as they were established in their jobs in Canada, however Frank suggested that they give it a try. Carolyn was able to take a leave of absence, and applied to teach in Broward County. Frank went down first and Carolyn followed two months later. He was able to find non-union work immediately.

During their time there they noticed the increased anxiety on both of their parts, fearing what the future might bring, completely aware that the time would come when they would not be able to manage on their own. At times they were the object of their anger and frustration. Frank bore the brunt of it, since it was usually related to family issues beyond anyone's control. One did not argue with Oma. They also noticed large gaps in Opa's memory.

While there, they walked Opa through his cataract surgery for both eyes and hoped he would be able to get his license back. His drivers' license was not renewed. He seemed to lose interest in many things and was unable to read as he had before. Having sold their four plex to a Hungarian couple, Frank and Carolyn rented one of their one-bedroom units, in the six-plex on NE 56th Court, for six months. Finding that wages were half what they had been earning in Canada and working conditions were not favorable for either of them, as a result, they told Oma and Opa they could not continue working and living in Florida. Understanding, but clearly disappointed, they agreed with their decision. They returned to Canada to help out with their daughter's wedding.

They arranged senior transportation and purchased a three-wheel tricycle for Oma with a large basket, hoping she could use it to go to the grocery store nearby. They tended to solicit the help of friends to take them to appointments and shopping.

Since Opa was not able to keep up with the apartments, he and Oma proposed that they be handed over to Frank or John or both together. Considering their different natures, Frank offered the apartments to John, with him buying Frank out. Unable to do that, Frank and Carolyn bought out John's interest at a price determined by three appraisals. It was also suggested that the apartments be sold, however Opa was not at all pleased with that option as he wanted them to be kept within the family. Transfer was completed with the help of Opa's lawyer, Fred Schmunk, in 1992. Oma wanted John to have more so $10,000 was added to the price. Opa also asked Frank to handle all their bills, so the addresses were changed, forwarding mail to their daughter's address in Lewiston, New York, thereby reducing time of delivery and the need for additional postage to Canada.

Chapter 9

※

The call came early in the morning, the time of day when you know it can only be bad news. This call was a call of desperation felt by Frank's parents, in need of support and no one near to help them. It is called the sandwich generation, caught between adult children struggling to get ahead and parents changing from an independent to a dependent role, both generations fighting change every step of the way. This middle generation in turn, struggles with feelings of love, loyalty, guilt, denial, and helplessness, hoping events will quickly find resolution. Oma quietly said hello and sobbing overtook her. Handing the phone to Frank, he tried to calm her down to figure out exactly was going on. Having moved to Florida twenty years ago, they enjoyed good health, good weather and seldom phoned, since "it costs so much". A phone call was not a normal occurrence.

The grandchildren grew up not really knowing their grandparents, apart from their annual trip in August, to spend a week with each of their sons' families. They remained distant and somewhat removed, from family events. Now, however they were about to move to the front and center. Oma requested that he fly to Florida as soon as possible. Since Frank worked in construction and in that time, work was slowing down, he was able to get time off to respond to his parents' request. A mixture of feelings arose in Carolyn as she admired his strong sense of duty and supported the decisions he made on their behalf. He was able to sort out all the issues they faced at that time and returned home ten days later.

Both Oma and Opa's health situations began to deteriorate further. Oma was scheduled for "cleaning out her arteries" she called it. As it turned out, she had triple by-pass surgery and a valve replacement. She had surgery on June 24th and Carolyn flew to Florida to help them June 28th when the school year ended.

Gerda picked her up at the airport and they went directly to their home. Upon arrival, Opa, a lost soul, was unable to cope, without Oma. He seemed relieved to have her there to cook, clean and drive him to the hospital every day to visit Oma. She was in ICU for a full two weeks because she had developed an infection following surgery. Fortunately, they had Humana Gold Plus Health Care Plan and all costs were covered. She appreciated cool wash cloths, lotion on her hands and any news Carolyn could bring. She was extremely weak.

Patients remembering experiences during surgery may seem unorthodox, however, Oma shared an incredible one. Knowing her, as having a very straight forward approach to life, in general, her account telling, gives credence to the event. Placed under heavy and deep sedation for the triple bypass and valve replacement surgery, the doctor told them later that her heart had stopped and she was considered "gone" for perhaps about three minutes. Times are approximate of course. They had to shock her heart to get it started…now to Oma's side: Lying in bed in recovery after surgery, seeing a man in scrubs walk by, she became extremely agitated and with anger, said, "That's him, that's him, He's the one that raped me when I had my surgery." It took us some time to get her settled down. It was discovered later that he had been the one to administer the paddles, shocking her heart, bringing her back. She, however, perhaps hovering over, temporarily out of body, perceived it as act of rape. Near death experiences have been documented and it is a fascinating study. (eg. See the account of Eban Alexander III, Proof of Heaven) Oma had that experience.

Opa and Carolyn established a routine of driving to Hollywood every day. She settled him into a wheelchair at the door of the hospital, since he was unsteady on his feet, while she parked the car. It was a long trip to Oma's room which was in a distant wing. Despite the 90-degree weather outside, carrying a sweater was necessary, as it was so cool inside. He seemed to have moments reminiscent of his old self, as he suggested that perhaps she should be paying for the gas needed to drive there. That was her first indication that logic seemed to be absent in his thinking.

She asked Gerda to go out for dinner with her one evening, since she had been there to help Oma and Opa so many times and would likely be called upon in the future, as their needs were increasing rapidly. Gerda shared the story of Opa's car accident. Having his license taken away, Gerda would come over and take them, in their car, to doctor appointments. Upon returning home from one such day, Opa said he would drive the car into the carport, after all were out of the car. It was awkward getting out of the car when it was inside the carport, so Gerda, not wanting to create any issue, complied with his wishes. Oma and Gerda entered the house through the door in the carport and then on into the kitchen. Opa started the car up, proceeding into the carport and rather than hitting the brakes, hit the gas, dislodging the wall and hitting the hot water tank behind that wall. Mayhem resulted. Water everywhere, Oma shouting at Opa and he stood bewildered, saying, "Did I do that?" Bless Gerda, she found the shut off valve for the water line and reduced the damage. It was so fortunate that neither Oma nor Gerda was in the breezeway, behind the carport, or personal injury would have been the result. Oma and Opa hadn't given them full details about what had happened, so it was good to know the story. Carolyn called Frank to let him know how serious the situation had become.

When arriving back at Oma and Opa's house after the dinner with Gerda, Opa was in quite a state, he was not coherent, all the lights were on in the house. He was trying the apartment keys in their front door, completely frustrated. Carolyn was gradually able to distract him and calm him down.

Opa had a key case with loops in it to hold the keys in place. For some reason he wanted the front door key moved from the middle, to the end position, so she moved it for him. He then asked where the middle key was and started searching in the drawers for the missing key. He didn't understand that he had requested it be moved in the first place.

He wore elastic stockings to alleviate the pain from varicose veins and he started looking for them in his sock drawer. He emptied out his drawer putting them all on his bed. He finally found a pair, then put on a regular pair of socks. At 8:30, when he wanted to go to bed, he came to her and said, "Karen, (that was what they called me), there are socks all over my bed, what should I do with them?". She helped him put them back in his drawer so he could go to bed.

Another day, he got angry with her, saying she had changed the locks and mixed up his keys, and what was she doing there…. That was when she told him she would be returning to Canada. It was not up to her to take on the responsibility at that point. Being fully aware of the seriousness of his condition and that his care as well as Oma's were both top priorities for their sons to sort out. She had been there two full weeks and was exhausted. Since Opa wandered at night, restful sleep was not possible. With Oma set to come out of the hospital and go into rehab, John was called to come down from Cleveland to see what was going on.

John arrived the day Carolyn was to fly home and she updated him on health procedures, medications etc. It was a relief to hand the baton to him. Both Frank and John were accustomed to the idiosyncrasies of their parents. Many times, they would speak only German and she had no idea what they wanted, although body language was usually clear enough. It was completely understandable that their lives were changing rapidly and it was stressing them out considerably. Everyone was trying to do their best and it was difficult to find out what they really wanted and what they were willing to accept. As it turned out, Oma refused to stay at the rehab center, so John brought her home. After ten difficult days he returned to Cleveland leaving the two of them on their own. They refused help from anyone except family. Becoming aware of this, Frank called Home Health Services. As their situation became more desperate, they finally agreed to home care three days a week. Their conditions steadily worsened. On a Wednesday Frank received a call from a Social Worker stating that they needed twenty-four-hour care and that they were ready to enter a senior home. Concern and relief filled their hearts, since Carolyn was still on summer break, another flight was booked to Florida, four days this time.

She wrestled with many feelings, worry and empathy for the difficulties of families so far apart when problems arise. Will they like the home? Will she be strong enough to leave them if they are unhappy? Will she remember to do all the things that must be put in order until seeing them again? Will the financial arrangements work out? Fortunately, remembering to pack a novel for the flight and conscious that she would be facing a roller coaster of emotions in three hours, it felt good to get lost in its storyline.

Gerda picked her up at the airport and went directly to their home. They seemed relieved to see her and were willing to leave everything in her hands. That night their things were packed, under the direction of Oma, as she called out from her bed, including various items she felt necessary. The following morning at 10 am they sat in the office of a beautiful home in Lauderhill. The entrance looked like a hotel lobby in soft pastels. Large green plants and flowered comfortable furniture filled the room. The building smelled fresh and clean and laughter could be heard in the halls. After reading and signing numerous forms they were escorted to their individual private rooms. Oma insisted on separate rooms as she reported he would not let her sleep and he talked all the time. The rooms were carpeted and decorated in rose, gray and burgundy. The doors and standing wardrobes were massive and two easy chairs made visiting comfortable. A large private bathroom, hospital bed, a desk, large lamps, a table and floral print pictures on the walls created the illusion of a fine hotel room. The window overlooked a large green open field. Oma quickly climbed into bed, relief at last. Opa was settled in his room down the hall. He seemed confused and asked why he wasn't with Oma. After fifty-seven years of marriage, apart from her only for her surgery and during the war, they had never been separated.

The next three days were busy, ordering a phone for them, redirecting their mail, buying underwear, nightwear, slippers etc, bringing in their tv, labelling their clothes, cleaning their home, emptying the refrigerators, informing friends where they were, and just what she needed, renting a car, when theirs broke down right in the middle of a very busy day. She visited them each day informing them of what had been done and seeing if they had any other matters that needed attention. She continuously reassured them that this would be the best for them for the next while, and they settled in. In spite of many lists and frequent calls to Frank, nights were sleepless and headaches were all too prevalent. Two open seats next to her on the flight home allowed her to sleep most of the way.

A few years later, their dear friend, Gerda, was diagnosed with breast cancer and underwent a double mastectomy. She also recounted an experience, similar to Oma's. While under heavy sedation. She stated she saw both her parents and her partner, Warren, all sitting around in a lovely room, all holding gifts for her and inviting her to join them. They had all passed away several years before. She said, although tempted to join them, told them she wasn't ready to join them right now. She spoke of the very good feeling she had encountered and felt completely at peace during the encounter, having no fear. Such accounts may provide comfort, feeling the other side is one of tranquility and fulfillment. She moved to an ocean condo in Hillsboro Beach and passed away shortly after.

Chapter 10

❋

C hristmas found Frank and Carolyn back in Florida, once again and at the senior home, checking them out, to return home. Both were anxious to see their home, however neither were in any shape to remain there. Oma had little energy to do more than eat and sleep and Opa was confused even more. He had forgotten how to get dressed, spoke German all the time and retold stories as if they were present reality. Frank found it hard to clean and shower his father and tearfully recalled the man he used to be. Oma seemed angry with life and begged them to stay. Aware that the care they both needed was beyond both of them, they readmitted them a week later. Oma seemed somewhat pleased that meals would be once again punctual and offered a variety not afforded during her stay in their home with them. Once again, this daughter-in-law, had not quite measured up. This time, she didn't mind at all, with the knowledge they would have the care and supervision they needed. The struggle to do the right thing, while at the same time present options for their choice, created a balancing act difficult to maintain in the midst of emotional warfare. Frank had a way of calming the waters, perhaps because they trusted him so completely.

A lovely location, Heartland, worked out really well for them in the long run, 2599 NW 55th Avenue. Each having their own room was the best plan, as their needs were so different and all medications were monitored. Oma's diabetes was frequently checked and insulin levels were adjusted accordingly. They would join each other for meals. Since Opa tended to wander, he was placed in a secure wing which Oma could access, so she went over to his room to visit when she gained strength. Although concerned about the costs, Frank reassured them that they could afford it and need not worry about what would remain as inheritance. Their money was for their use. Being a Humana facility, all Doctor costs were covered however medications ran about $500 per month and each paid $100 per day for room, meals and nursing care. Oma tended to sleep a great deal, which her body needed, after such invasive surgery.

A friend provided guidance as she told them to make decisions for them out of inspiration rather than desperation and to take comfort in the knowledge, they were doing the best they could, for their loved ones. The emotional journey taken was inevitable and it was hoped there would be a smooth transition for their future experience.

In the US, financial and health care are arranged differently than in Canada, it was explained to them, at that time, that the future could hold the complete depletion of all of Oma and Opa's assets, savings, home etc. Once that was all gone, however, there was comfort in the knowledge that they will be able to stay in the same home, when the cupboard was bare. The home would use their social security, as payment and they will not be required to make another move. Fortunately, it didn't come to that conclusion, so we didn't see, if that was the reality of the situation.

Frank phoned every Sunday to check in with Oma and Carolyn continued communication with the administrators regarding their needs and medical status. They handled all the bills for them. Frank let John know the situation and he suggested that they come to Cleveland and stay in the German senior home there. It was suggested to Oma and Opa, but Oma didn't agree to that option. Opa was diagnosed with "senile dementia". He was happy in his world and compliant with whatever was decided. It was so fortunate that Oma had a very clear, sharp understanding of the difficulties facing them and took on the responsibility of making all major decisions for both of them. Oma decided she needed to be closer to family and it was left up to her to make the choice, Cleveland or Niagara Falls. With that focus, they returned home, hoping for the best.

Frank spoke clearly to Oma that a decision to move was completely up to her and she indicated that her first choice was to move to Cleveland, where she could live with her brother, Joe, and Opa could have care at the senior home where Joe's wife, Maria(Mitzi) worked at the end of their street.

With a plan in place, HMO health care plans in Ohio were researched, since Humana was not there and a transfer would not be possible. Kaiser Permanente was available, with a similar plan to what they had had and all the documentation was completed for the move. They didn't have any interruption in care or medications.

Although it was March, it was still quite cold in Ohio and Opa didn't have any winter coat, so Frankie was asked to meet them at the Cleveland airport, loaning him one of his, for the trip to the senior home now called Diplomat Healthcare, 9001 W 130th Street in North Royalton. On the flight, sitting next to Frank, he looked out the window at the clouds, and with child-like wonderment said, "There is a lot of snow down there." In many ways, he was almost better off, since, as long as his immediate needs were met, he was content to watch the world go by. After Opa was settled into his room, having made all the arrangements in advance, they took Oma over to Joe and Mitzi's home. They had prepared the guest bedroom for her and she went immediately to bed to rest as the day had been very tiring, to say the least.

51

Chapter 11

❖

Frank and Carolyn stayed overnight with Frankie, at his home in Gates Mills. Returning the following day, to say goodbye to Oma, before driving home to Canada, they were met with a surprise. Joe stated that he would be charging his sister $60 per day for her room and board as that was the going rate for assisted living. Oma was shocked, however without any alternative, she had to accept his conditions. Since Frank was POA for Oma and Opa and paying all their bills, he prepared a monthly check on behalf of Oma. It wasn't an issue for him, since it was their money and their care, that was of paramount importance and he knew Oma would benefit from Mitzi's good meals and a safe environment.

Frank spoke to his mother every Sunday and they would make the trip to Cleveland, once a month, to visit both of them. Opa developed bowel cancer and had surgery to remove a section of his large intestine. He was amazing, in that, upon his return to the senior home after surgery, expecting he would be in bed for a while, to everyone's surprise, he got up and was walking around the next day. Oma visited him each day, bringing him baked treats, which he always enjoyed. After eight months, Oma called us and told us she wanted both of them to come to Canada as soon as possible. She didn't disclose her plan to Joe and upon our usual monthly visit, she announced to them that they would be leaving with us that weekend.

Beforehand, unaware of the change of location, John had her sign a document revoking Frank's POA. He provided him with a copy and after reading it, Frank quickly called a German speaking lawyer to explain the implications to Oma. He understood it, however didn't want to be responsible for her understanding. Marlene Strugg, a lawyer with the German Club in Cleveland, fortunately gave them an appointment and Oma was able to revoke the document, back to Frank once again. She had had no understanding of what she had signed.

At one point, with great frustration, Frank said to his brother, "Please take over, it is not an easy job. Your help would be welcomed". Oma told us afterwards she almost had another heart attack thinking Frank would not be there for support.

Frank let John know Oma's wishes regarding the move to Canada and he then came over to Frankie's home and wanted to discuss money with Frank. It was apparent that he did not trust him. He told him that Oma didn't have to be present. Frank responded that indeed she needed to be present, since it was their money, he wanted to discuss. When Oma understood John's request, she replied, "I am still here. I don't know how long I will live, nor how much I will need." That ended the discussion and it was made clear that their wills were a 50-50 split that would be handled through all the appropriate channels upon their passing, wherever they lived.

Previously, hearing her wishes, Frank and Carolyn had contacted their member of Parliament about procedures to sponsor parents, returning to Canada from the US. They were American citizens and they were instructed that they would need to apply at the Canadian consulate in Cleveland and that it would take some time. Fortunately, they were also advised due to their health needs and no one else to look after them, they could enter Canada with them, as visitors, and apply after being here for a period of time. This was a special consideration due to their age and needs. Frank told the member that they would not be any financial burden for the country and could pay their way without any difficulty. That didn't matter, however they followed their advice and brought them over the border as guests.

Initially, Oma lived with them and they found a place for Opa. They were both working full time and he was in need of care, bathing, toileting etc. When returning home from school, Carolyn would drive Oma over to see Opa, a short distance from their home. She was charged with the duties, morning and night, of giving Oma her insulin shots and testing her sugar levels to ascertain the dosage of insulin needed. It was a responsibility that she was ill prepared for and certainly not qualified for. Opa was in distress since Oma wasn't by his side and got out of the facility and wandered over to the motel next door, knocking on the doors calling for Eva. They were informed that he needed a secure facility and not the assisted living situation that had been chosen. With a need to change, they researched various homes.

They also investigated homes near the US border, since they were enrolled in Blue Cross in New York State. It was felt in the event hospitalization might become necessary they could be transported over the bridge to Buffalo General. A lovely place, in Fort Erie, The Residence on Garrison Road was selected. Here Oma joined Opa, having her own room, Opa in the secure wing, having all meals together and Oma able to go over to his secure wing to check on him at any time. She was happy with the arrangement and costs were one half what they had paid in Florida for the same supports. All the medications could be brought in and they were pleased that the number of meds that the doctor recommended for both of them, was decreased significantly. After six months there, they had a surprise in that the home had made application, unknown to them, for Ontario Medical Insurance, on their behalf, and coverage was granted.

Chapter 12

❈

They were so fortunate that Oma was completely clear and could make all her own decisions, as money issues arose and the trust factor was quickly squashed by her, every time. She was kept abreast of the financial status and she made it clear, information was to be kept confidential. Life began to develop a quiet routine. Visiting them three times a week and excursions on Sundays pleased them. They enjoyed themselves and were tired out at the end of a day and happy to return to their comfortable rooms. The care they received was excellent. Initially, Oma played the "poor me" position, however they knew it wasn't accurate. The recreation director, Alicia, being the daughter of one of the secretaries, where Carolyn taught, told her mom that Oma was a social butterfly, visiting the other ladies, having tea with them and proudly share pictures of the family to anyone interested. She had found a social network that helped the time go by. Opa was doing well, happy in his own world. He needed assistance with all self-care, showering etc. and the staff was wonderful with him.

Frank was invited to a class reunion, in 1993, in Germany, and with his parents doing so well, they decided to take the three-week trip to Germany and Hungary.

Toward the end of their trip, they received a call from their daughter, telling them that Opa was in the hospital with pneumonia. Upon our return, he was in a very weakened state and he passed away shortly after. Family was notified. Joe and his son, Ronald and John and Betty from Cleveland, attended the funeral, along with the friends from Europe, that lived in Canada. It seemed to be the end of an era. Eleven months later, Oma, having diabetes, had developed a sore on one of her feet and amputation was suggested. The infection blackened her foot and the doctor recommended that her lower leg be removed asap. Before that surgery, she had a stroke on a Tuesday and then another on Friday, the second one, taking her life. She had found without Opa, life had lost its purpose and seemed resigned with the idea of joining him.

After Opa passed, Frank asked Oma where she wanted him to be buried. Having lived in Hungary, Germany, Canada and the US, it was important that she make that decision. She thought about it for about a week and told him that since Opa was so close to his mother, perhaps Hungary, at his parents' gravesite. They were able to transport both their ashes to Vertesboglar and they were interred with his parents. Bela had the stone redone with their names and it was a lovely beige marble above ground level plot, similar to what can be seen in New Orleans. Each country has such different traditions. They were together once again.

Conclusion

❈

They were two peas in a pod, one could not be without the other. Finishing each other's sentences, anticipating the other's needs and constantly teasing one another. In light of their history, they were a testament of unity, strength, love, ambition, energy and caring generous people, in spite of all the odds.

This is what Canada and the United States consists of, strong immigrants, people willing to give their all, for a better life, for themselves and for their families.

Carolyn has in her possession a tattered recipe book of Oma's, spattered with spots of batter, unfortunately written in Hungarian, the baking secrets scribbled within, remaining hidden, never to appear in her kitchen. Her talents are remembered and were appreciated by many.

Attending New Year's Eve dances in Florida, a dance with Opa, meant that one was swept around the floor, as he practically lifted you off your feet. It seemed one was floating around the dance floor, strong and confident, many times dancing and singing the songs that he knew so well.

They are missed. While sitting together in the seniors' home, Opa turned to Oma and said, "Holt meine Werkzeuge fangen wir weider an." (Get my tools, we will start again.) Bless them in their new beginning.

Abraham-Hicks put it succinctly, "The basis of life is freedom, the purpose of life is joy, the result of life is growth."

Opa was proud to say, "I earned a living with a hammer, my son, with a screwdriver and my grandson, with a pencil."

Freedom is sweet when you have known bondage. Joy is sweet when you have known sorrow. Everyone grows with this ever-expanding universe. Life is an adventure. Contrast and diversity make life interesting.

We are so blessed to live in this time of history and in a place of plenty.

A small collection of historical memorabilia has been appended, as a tribute to their fascinating and meandering life stories, along with a brief record of some of the ancestry accompanied by a collection of photos.

Appendix 1

❈

S hort narrative regarding Vertesboglar, as shared in a letter from Joseph Stiftinger, to George Stiftinger, first cousin to Frank(Opa)

"From Dec 21 to Jan 8 we were on vacation. During this time, I collected more information about our ancestors. In Budapest, at the National Szechenji Library. I found a book that deals with the Donauswaben. The author, Antal Taffener, was born at Vertesboglar and this book deals with Vertesboglar exclusively. The author finished grade school at Vertesboglar and high school and his studies at the University of Budapest. His first book published in 1941, deals with immigrants to Vertesboglar.

Initially, the place was called Boglar and consisted of a sheep-sty and sheep-herder's house. It belonged to Count Esterhasi who lived in the neighboring village called Csokvar. The first immigrants appeared in 1755 on the Count's property, and were from Baden-Wurttemberg, Germany. By 1760 they had built a small village.

The author found a contract, from that time that showed very hard agreements: each week they must work one day for the Count, and since their place was at Vertes Mountain, each must clear 2 hold, about 4 acres of forest, just in order to have the right to build a house. In order to build a house (get the material) they had to work additionally in the forest and brick factory.

The cleared land was poor and the great amount of work disenchanted a lot of immigrants and they moved to Banat, presently Yugoslavia. A Marienfeld Church record in the Czech Republic, showed people who were born in Vertesboglar.

A pestilence at this time killed many: one grave a mother and her six children were buried together. Soon only five or six families existed.

A new group of immigrants came in 1760. These were of Bajor (Austrian) origin and the author proves this using names and words of Bajor origin. The Stiftinger name appears now, after the second migration."

Appendix 2

❈

History of the Miehle name:

Tracing from Opa's parents back in time:

His father and mother were Joannes Miehle(1875-1925) and Anna Stiftinger(1876-1959) married the winter of the year 1900. They had four children: Janos(1903-1961)) born in Sharon, Pennsylvania, married to Rosa Kluger, Anna (1905-1946) born in Vertesboglar, married to Johann Herczig, Ferenz(1908-1993) Opa born in Vertesboglar married to Eva Hanek, and Paul(1918-1969) born in Vertesboglar, married to Klara Trauker. Occupation of father- Butcher. Place of birth of father-Budaors, Hungary.

Opa's paternal grandparents: Gyorgy (Georgius) (1847) and Susanna Grosz: Occupation of father-wagon maker. Place of birth of father Budakeszi, Hungary. They had two children Theresa(Winkler) and Joannes.

Opa's paternal great grandparents: Josephus Mille and Teresia Eszterle (1826): Place of birth of father-Budakeszi, Hungary.

Opa's paternal great, great grandparents: Josephur Mihle/ Mille(1790)Elisabetha Merkl Place of father's birth-Budakeszi, Hungary

Opa's paternal great, great, great grandparents: Joannes Felix Mille and Catharina Krenin/Krenn: Place of birth of father. Budakeszi area.

Opa's great, great, great, great grandparents Xaverius Mille and Theresia. Place of birth of father: Germany Baden-Wurttemberg area.

Appendix 3

❖

Records of Oma's family: according to accounts provided by Lisie Dien in the 1970's.

Eva Hanek (Oma)'s parents were: John Hanek(1891-1966) and Anna Kellner (1891-1960) Their children were: Eva(1914-1994), Anna(1915-1979), Joseph(1930-2014) Both parents were born in Vesces, Hungary and passed away in Riechenbach, Germany.

Eva's father had four sisters: Luisi (Scarley), John second born, Maria (Granosty), Theresa (?), and Rosa(Fruhwirth)

Eva's mother, Anna, had five sisters and two brothers: Rosa(Probstl)1884, Theresa(Strohmeyer)1886, Rosalia(Fruhwirth)1889, Anna fourth born,1891, Maria(Zehetmayer)1894, Elizabeth(Dien)1896, Ferdinand Kellner,1900, and Thomas Kellner,1903.

Records and photos

Family Kellner

Oma's grandparents on
her mother's side-Kellner

At Oma's grandfather's funeral.

L-R : Thomas Kellner, Terezia Strohmayer, Rosa Probstl, Ferdinand Kellner, Rosalia Fruhwiert, Anna Hanek, Elizabeth Dien, Maria Zehetmayer-Zala(Hungarianized), Kellner-Karpoty(Hungarianized)

Anna Kellner and John Hanek, wedding picture

Anna Kellner(1891), John Hanek(1891),(Parents)and Eva Hanek(1914)standing,
Anna Hanek(1915)

Center, Anna Stiftinger(1876), to her right, her husband, John Miehle(1875) Sharon, Pennsylvania.

Anna Stiftinger and John Miehle and first born, Johann(1903)

Anna Stiftinger and John Miehle, at their daughter's wedding, Anna and Johann Herczig

John Hanek, standing on left, his wife, Anna Kellner, third over in middle row. Hungary.

Johann Miehle(1903) and wife, Rosa Kluber(1908) with Johann(1928) Bela(1932)

Frank Miehle(1908) sitted, brother Johann Miehle(1903) standing.

Frank Miehle and Eva Hanek's wedding(1934), boy standing on left in front, Joseph Hanek(1930), Eva's little brother.

Eva and Frank walking to festival

Wedding portrait Frank and Eva

Frank Miehle(1936)

Eva Hanek, Frank Jr, and father, Frank Miehle, in yard at their home .

John Miehle(1942) Eva, Frank(1936) and father Frank Miehle, just before the war.

Miehle family after the war, in Germany.

Family in Germany, living there from 1946 to 1953.

John and Frank playing accordian on Zeppelin Strasse, Denkendorf, Germany.

Eight-family house in Denkendorf, Germany.

Frank's soccer teams while in Denkendorf.

Frank happy with a soccer ball.

Gathering of his classmates prior to immigration to Canada, 1953.

Führerschein

für

Herrn
Fräulein *Franz Miehle*

geboren am *21. Mai 1908*

in *Vertesboglar / Ungarn*

wohnhaft in *Denkendorf*

Kreis Eßlingen

*Deinweiler*straße Nr. *45*

Herr
Fräulein *Franz Miehle*

erhält die Erlaubnis, nach Ablegung der Prüfung ein Kraftfahrzeug
mit Antrieb durch *Verbrennungsmaschine*

der Klasse *3/drei* zu führen.

Erteilung am *den 6. Dezember* 195*1*

Landratsamt
Des Bezirkes

Regierungsoberrat
(Bezeichnung der Behörde und Unterschrift)

Lfd. Nr. *RO 599*
Gebühr: 3 DM Reg. Nr 2396
Nach bestandener Prüfung ausgehändigt.

Nürtingen den *17. Januar* 195*2*

Der amtlich anerkannte Sachverständige

(Unterschrift)

Kennkarte Nr. *WD - 537/358*

Eigenhändige Unterschrift des Inhabers:

BUNDESREPUBLIK DEUTSCHLAND
FEDERAL REPUBLIC OF GERMANY
RÉPUBLIQUE FÉDÉRALE D'ALLEMAGNE

Gebührenmarke
Fiscal stamp
Droit de timbre

REISEPASS
PASSPORT
PASSEPORT

Nr. B 6373307

Michle

Name des Paßinhabers / Name et bearer / Nom du titulaire

Franz

Vornamen / Christian names / Prénoms

Begleitet von seiner Ehefrau
Accompanied by his wife
Accompagné de sa femme

Eva Michle

geb. Hanex

und   Kindern
and   children
et de   enfants

Staatsangehörigkeit: **Deutsche**
Nationality
Nationalité

Reg.-Nr.
Registration No.   *185 / 1965*
Nº d'enregistrement

Dieser Paß enthält 32 Seiten / This passport contains 32 pages / Ce passeport contient 32 pages

Zur Beachtung

1. Der Personalausweis ist auf Verlangen allen Behörden sowie den Beamten des Polizeidienstes vorzuzeigen.

2. Es ist strafbar, den Inhalt des Personalausweises zu entstellen oder ihn in seinem Inhalt zu verändern, den Personalausweis einem andern zum Gebrauch zu überlassen oder einen fremden Personalausweis zu benutzen.

3. Der Verlust ist der zur Ausstellung zuständigen Behörde des Wohnortes unverzüglich anzuzeigen.

4. Der Personalausweis gilt nur als Inlandsausweis.

Verlängert bis:

Unterschrift

BUNDESREPUBLIK DEUTSCHLAND

Personalausweis

Nummer des Personalausweises
BW 145 - 705

Gültig bis
15. 6. 1958

Name (bei Ehefrauen auch Geburtsname)
Miehle geb. Hanek

Vornamen (Rufnamen unterstreichen)
Eva

Geburtstag
8. 1. 1914

Geburtsort (Land, Kreis)
Vecses/Budapest

Staatsangehörigkeit
deutsch

Größe
158 cm vollschlank

Farbe der Augen
hellbraun

Unveränderliche Kennzeichen
keine

Miehle, Eva
Unterschrift des Inhabers

Denkendorf 15. 6. 1953
Datum

Unterschrift des ausstellenden Beamten

Wohnort (ggf. Wohnung
Denkendorf
Deizisauerstr.

Zugezogen in (Wohnort und Wohnung)

Oberbehörde

Zugezogen in (Wohnort und Wohnung)

Oberbehörde

Sept. 18, 1953 aboard the freighter, Castelbianco on voyage to Halifax, Canada

PIER 21
SHIPS

AROSA KULM

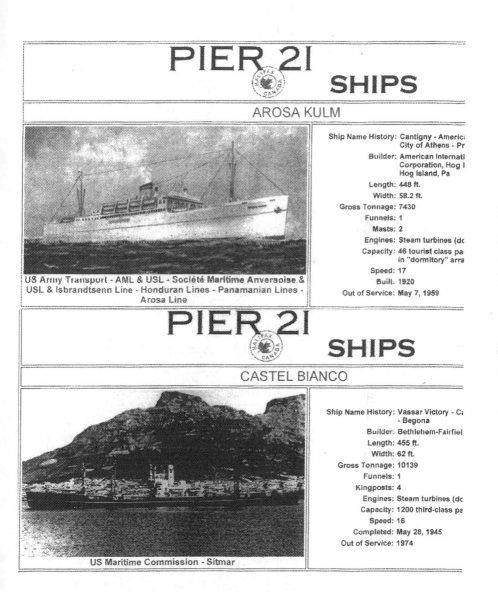

Ship Name History: Cantigny - America
City of Athens - Pr
Builder: American Internatl
Corporation, Hog I
Hog Island, Pa
Length: 448 ft.
Width: 58.2 ft.
Gross Tonnage: 7430
Funnels: 1
Masts: 2
Engines: Steam turbines (dc
Capacity: 46 tourist class pa
in "dormitory" arra
Speed: 17
Built: 1920
Out of Service: May 7, 1959

US Army Transport - AML & USL - Société Maritime Anversoise &
USL & Isbrandtsenn Line - Honduran Lines - Panamanian Lines -
Arosa Line

PIER 21
SHIPS

CASTEL BIANCO

Ship Name History: Vassar Victory - Ca
- Begona
Builder: Bethlehem-Fairfiel
Length: 455 ft.
Width: 62 ft.
Gross Tonnage: 10139
Funnels: 1
Kingposts: 4
Engines: Steam turbines (dc
Capacity: 1200 third-class pa
Speed: 16
Completed: May 28, 1945
Out of Service: 1974

US Maritime Commission - Sitmar

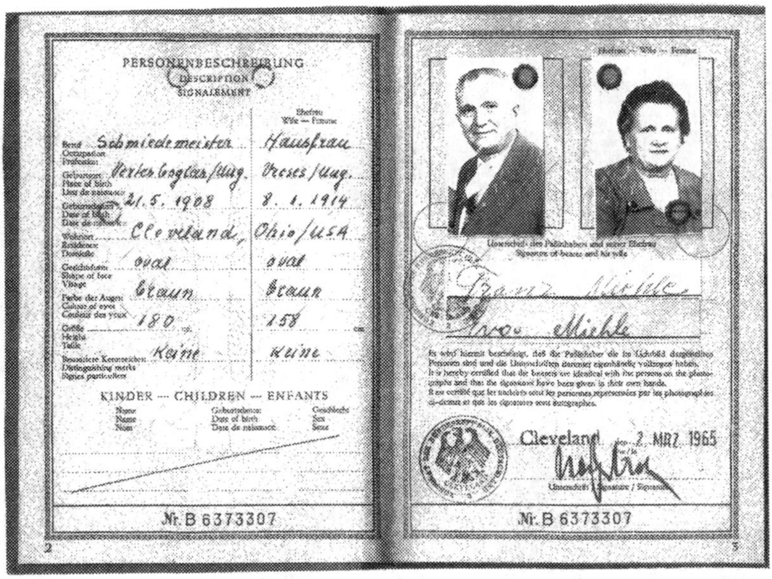

PERSONENBESCHREIBUNG
DESCRIPTION
SIGNALEMENT

		Ehefrau Wife — Femme
Beruf Occupation Profession	Schmiedemeister	Hausfrau
Geburtsort Place of birth Lieu de naissance	Vester Coglas/Ung.	Oroses/Ung.
Geburtstag Date of birth Date de naissance	21.5.1908	8.1.1914
Wohnort Residence Domicile	Cleveland,	Ohio/USA
Gesichtsform Shape of face Visage	oval	oval
Farbe der Augen Colour of eyes Couleur des yeux	braun	braun
Größe Height Taille	180 cm	158 cm
Besondere Kennzeichen Distinguishing marks Signes particuliers	keine	keine

KINDER — CHILDREN — ENFANTS

Name Name Nom	Geburtsdatum Date of birth Date de naissance	Geschlecht Sex Sexe

Nr. B 6373307

2

Ehefrau · Wife · Femme

Unterschrift des Paßinhabers und seiner Ehefrau
Signature of bearer and his wife

Franz Miehle

Frau Miehle

Es wird hiermit bescheinigt, daß der Paßinhaber die im Lichtbild dargestellten Personen sind und die Unterschriften darunter eigenhändig vollzogen haben.
It is hereby certified that the bearer is identical with the persons on the photographs and that the signatures have been given in their own hands.
Il est certifié que les porteurs sont les personnes représentées par les photographies ci-dessus et que les signatures sont autographes.

Cleveland, den 2. MRZ 1965

Unterschrift / Signature / Signature

Nr. B 6373307

3

Frank and Eva's home on Atlee Street, Niagara Falls, Ontario.

Frank and Eva's home on Lloyd Road, Cleveland, Ohio.

Frank and Eva's home in Fort Lauderdale, Florida

New Year's party Florida

Oma and Opa's graves in Vertesboglar, Hungary, with Opa's parents.

Bela Miehle, Carolyn Miehle, Ferenz Herczig, In front of Opa's birthplace. Vertesboglar.

BUNDESREPUBLIK DEUTSCHLAND
FEDERAL REPUBLIC OF GERMANY
RÉPUBLIQUE FÉDÉRALE D'ALLEMAGNE

Gebührenmarke
Fiscal stamp
Droit de timbre

REISEPASS
PASSPORT
PASSEPORT

Nr. B 6373307

Miehle
Name des Paßinhabers / Name of bearer / Nom du titulaire

Franz
Vorname / Christian name / Prénom

Begleitet von seiner Ehefrau
Accompanied by his wife
Accompagné de sa femme

Eva Miehle

geb. Hanck

und
and
et de
Kinder
children
enfants

Staatsangehörigkeit
Nationality
Nationalité
Deutsche

Reg.-Nr.
Registration No.
Nº d'enregistrement
185 / 1960

Dieser Paß enthält 32 Seiten / This passport contains 32 pages / Ce passeport contient 32 pages

Printed in the United States
by Baker & Taylor Publisher Services